Who Bit My Tail?

Tiger was fast asleep dreaming about chasing a rat.

Snap snap went Tiger's teeth, biting at the rat's tail!

-t-t-t-t-t-t-t-t-t-t-t-t-t-t-t-t-t-t-t-

Tiger woke up feeling happy.

Wha**t** a grea**t** dream!

He stretched ou**t** his paws and claws.

He stretched ou**t** his legs and **t**ail ...

What was this?

Tiger's tail had been bitten!

There were big bite marks near the tip of his tail.

"Who bit my tail?" Tiger growled.

He went off in search of the biter.

Tiger found a tortoise.

"Tortoise, did you bite my tail?" asked Tiger.

"No Tiger, I didn't bite your tail, I don't have any teeth!"
Tortoise opened his mouth to show Tiger.

"Then who bit my tail?"

Tiger found a bat.

"Bat, did you bite my tail?" asked Tiger.

"No Tiger, I didn't bite your tail, my teeth are too small!" Bat opened his mouth to show Tiger.

"Then who bit my tail?"

Tiger found a goat.

"Goat, did you bite my tail?" asked Tiger.

"No Tiger, I didn't bite your tail, my teeth are too blunt!" Goat opened his mouth to show Tiger.

"Then who bit my tail?"

Tiger found a kitten.

"Kitten, you bit my tail!" Tiger said.

"No Tiger, I didn't bite your tail, my teeth are too tiny!" Kitten showed her teeth to Tiger.

"Then who bit my tail!?" Tiger cried.

Ki**tt**en looked hard at **T**iger's **t**ail.

"You were bi**tt**en by big **t**eeth – like yours!
You bi**t** your own **t**ail," said Ki**tt**en.

Tiger pu**t** his **t**eeth on the bi**t**e mark.

They fi**tt**ed perfectly.

"I bi**t** my own **t**ail!" **T**iger went brigh**t** red.

I**t** wasn't the ra**t** in **T**iger's dream a**t** all –
i**t** was his own **t**ail **T**iger bi**t**!